Wars at Home

(1812–1820)

by Michelle Quinby

LIGHTB◆X
openlightbox.com

LIGHTBOX

Go to
www.openlightbox.com
and enter this book's
unique code.

ACCESS CODE

L B X H 7 2 7 5

Lightbox is an all-inclusive digital solution for the
teaching and learning of curriculum topics in an original,
groundbreaking way. Lightbox is based on National
Curriculum Standards.

STANDARD FEATURES OF LIGHTBOX

 AUDIO High-quality
narration using text-to-
speech system

 ACTIVITIES Printable
PDFs that can be emailed
and graded

 SLIDESHOWS
Pictorial overviews
of key concepts

 VIDEOS Embedded high-
definition video clips

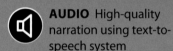 **WEBLINKS** Curated
links to external,
child-safe resources

 TRANSPARENCIES
Step-by-step layering of
maps, diagrams, charts,
and timelines

 INTERACTIVE MAPS
Interactive maps and
aerial satellite imagery

 QUIZZES Ten multiple
choice questions that
are automatically
graded and emailed for
teacher assessment

 KEY WORDS
Matching key concepts
to their definitions

Contents

Chapter One

Building American Pride

*The people who lived in the United States in the early 1800s were proud of their new country. However, most of them did not really think of themselves as Americans. Being an American was not that important to them. They had not yet developed a sense of **nationalism**.*

I n the late 1770s and early 1780s, Americans fought hard to win their independence from Great Britain. They worked together at that time in the American Revolutionary War. However, they did not really learn to identify one another as Americans and to believe in America as a great place. Now, they needed to build their country together. If the United States was going to be strong, Americans had to believe it could last. They had to be sure of their country's future.

Some things helped pull Americans together. They had important things in common. For example, they had made themselves new lives in North America. They loved freedom.

In the last major battle of the American Revolutionary War, British troops surrendered to the American forces led by George Washington at Yorktown, Virginia, in 1781.

George Washington was sworn in as president at Federal Hall in New York City in 1789.

Americans were hard-working people. They were brave. They shared a lot of beliefs, too. For example, most of them were Christians. In addition, they believed people should be equal. They thought that all white men should be equal, anyway. It would take quite a bit longer before women and people of other races were thought of the same way.

At first, Americans did not want to have anything to do with the rest of the world's business. George Washington, the first president of the United States, did not want Americans to get pulled into foreign wars. European countries, such as Great Britain and France, were often at war.

Washington worried that the United States was not strong enough to handle a war. He thought that Americans needed to pay attention to their own country first. However, by the time Thomas Jefferson, the third president, left office in 1809, Europe was a tense place. It had become hard to stay **neutral**.

Like America, France had gone through a revolution in the late 1700s. Then, Napoleon Bonaparte had taken over as ruler of France in 1799. The French were excited under his leadership. He wanted to take over the world.

The British did not want the French to become too strong. Great Britain had gone to war with France in 1803. The United States wanted to keep from taking sides. Americans did not want to get pulled into the conflict that became known as the Napoleonic Wars.

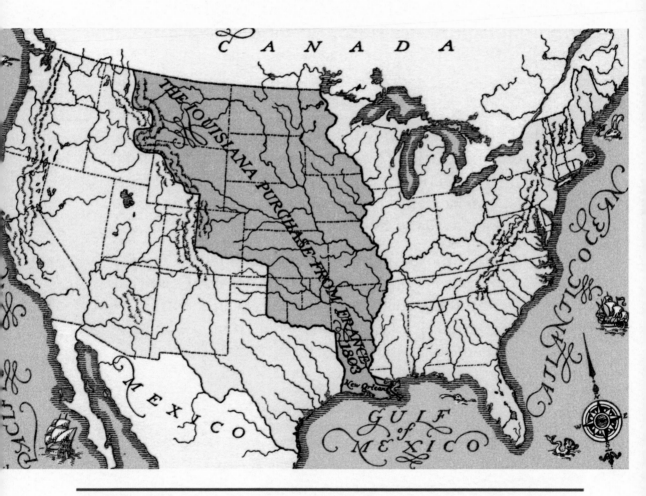

President Jefferson took advantage of France's need for money during the Napoleonic Wars to make the Louisiana Purchase. For $15 million, the United States bought 828 million square miles (2.1 billion square kilometers) of land, greatly increasing the country's size.

During the 12 years of the Napoleonic Wars, the French and British did not seem able to think of the United States as a "real" country, in charge of its land and water. European ships appeared on the U.S. coast. They seized American ships and sailors.

Many Americans were angered by these events. The way Great Britain and France treated the United States made the people in the United States draw closer together. They started to think of themselves as Americans. Their sense of nationalism was growing.

As president, Jefferson tried to force Great Britain and France to respect the United States. In 1807, he stopped all **trade** with those countries until they promised to leave the United States alone. He wanted them to agree that the United States could be neutral in the European war.

Stopping foreign trade did not work, though. Americans needed goods from France and Great Britain. They needed supplies for their factories. American businesses ended up being hurt more than European businesses. Americans started **smuggling** goods down through Canada to get what they needed.

James Madison, who became president after Jefferson, tried to get respect for the nation as well. In 1810, Congress passed a law that the United States could trade with European countries again. However, Congress also said that this would continue only if France or Great Britain allowed the United States to conduct trade as a neutral nation.

Some historians estimate that **5 million troops** and other people died in the Napoleonic Wars.

An **1807 British attack** on a U.S. ship left three American sailors dead and 18 wounded.

U.S. trade was worth **$108 million** in 1807 and **fell** to just **$22 million** in 1808.

In the early 1800s, British officers would often force captured American sailors to work on British ships.

Immediately, Napoleon said France would respect America's neutrality. However, British ships continued to stop U.S. vessels and force American sailors into service for Great Britain. So, President Madison stopped trade with Great Britain again. Meanwhile, the British were also moving in on American territory in the West. This made Americans even angrier. The British seemed to be saying that the United States was not a real country.

Americans disagreed about what they should do. Older people, who remembered the American Revolutionary War, did not want to fight more battles. They knew how bad war could be. Some younger leaders, though, such as Henry Clay and Andrew Jackson, pushed for war. They wanted to teach the British a lesson. They thought Americans should prove to Great Britain how strong they were. People called them the War Hawks, because they really wanted to fight.

Henry Clay, a member of Congress who favored war with Great Britain, later helped write the treaty to end the war.

The British finally promised to stop capturing American sailors. It was too late, though. Americans were mad at the British for trying to take land in the West. The British were banding together with some of the Native American groups. This scared many Americans.

The War Hawks had had enough. They persuaded Congress to start a war. In June of 1812, the United States went to war against Great Britain. This conflict became known as the War of 1812.

TECUMSEH'S MOVEMENT

Tecumseh's real name, his Native American name, was Tekamthi. He was born on March 9, 1768, as a shooting star streaked across the night sky. His father, a Shawnee chief, thought this was a sign of his son's greatness. As he grew up, Tekamthi saw how white settlers were moving west and pushing the Native Americans off their land.

Tekamthi wanted to find a way to live peacefully with the white settlers, but he also wanted to make sure his people did not lose their homes. He believed that if Native American groups stood together, they would be too strong for the white settlers to defeat. He said that one group of Native Americans by itself was like a single hair. The white people could easily snap it. Together, the Native Americans would be like a braid. They would be too strong to be broken.

By 1800, Tekamthi was a well-known Native American leader. He traveled across North America. He brought his message to all the Native peoples. His brother, a religious leader, went with him. People called them Tecumseh and the Prophet. The brothers even formed a capital for Native Americans, called Prophetstown, in Indiana. Before Tekamthi could pull Native groups together, though, the Americans stopped him. The U.S. army destroyed Prophetstown in 1811. In response, Tekamthi turned to the British for help. After all, they had the same goal. They both wanted to keep the United States from expanding. When the War of 1812 broke out, Tekamthi helped the British capture Detroit, in what is now Michigan. However, he was killed in battle in 1813.

Chapter Two

War with Great Britain

The United States was not really ready for a war. The American army had only 12,000 soldiers. Most of the officers did not have much experience leading troops in battle. Many Americans did not want the war. They thought it was a terrible idea. Other Americans, though, wanted to teach Great Britain a lesson. They wanted to prove that the United States could not be pushed around.

Canada was the United States' closest neighbor. It was not an independent country yet, though. It still belonged to Great Britain. The Americans knew they could best attack the British in Canada.

The U.S. fort on Mackinac Island, in Lake Huron, was captured by the British early in the War of 1812.

One group of American soldiers went into Canada through Detroit. Another crossed the Niagara River, which forms part of the border between western New York State and Canada. Farther east, a third group of soldiers crossed Lake Champlain and moved toward Montreal.

The Americans thought they would not have trouble invading Canada. Americans believed that the people living in Canada would be glad to be freed from Great Britain. They thought Canadians would want to join the United States. U.S. Army officers expected the Canadians to turn against the British and help them.

However, that's not what happened. Instead, the Americans lost badly. The British captured the city of Detroit. The troops who had crossed the Niagara River were quickly defeated. Those who had gone toward Montreal ended up refusing to fight.

A monument to Major General Isaac Brock, the British officer responsible for defeating the Americans in Detroit, stands in the city of Niagara, Canada.

The war was not only fought in or near Canada, though. The British had the best navy in the world. They brought more than 1,000 ships to block U.S. ports. They did not want the Americans to be able to get in or out. They did not want them to be able to do business with other countries. The Americans had only 14 ships. The fight did not look very fair. The British seemed likely to win at sea, as well.

Now used mainly for display, the USS *Constitution* is the oldest vessel in the U.S. Navy.

When the American ships fought the British in battle, though, they did very well. In one sea battle, the British shot their cannons at the USS *Constitution*. The cannonballs bounced off the ship's sides. "Her sides are made of iron!" shouted an American sailor. In fact, the ship was made of live oak, the hardest wood in the world, and the **hull** was 2 feet (0.6 meters) thick. That is why the cannonballs bounced off.

Americans were proud of their navy. They began calling the *Constitution* "Old Ironsides." The ship became a symbol of pride and hope.

The war started to drag on. The British were able to keep the Americans from using their seaports most of the time. U.S. businesses had a hard time getting the goods they needed. Americans had a difficult time, too.

The Americans were not able to invade Canada, but the British were not able to defeat the Americans completely, either. Meanwhile, in the West, American general William Henry Harrison was building an army. On the Great Lakes, U.S. naval officer Oliver Hazard Perry was putting together an inland navy. On September 10, 1813, Perry led his **fleet** in the Battle of Lake Erie.

Oliver Hazard Perry had to leave his damaged ship, the *Lawrence*, during the Battle of Lake Erie, but the U.S. fleet was still victorious under his leadership.

The Battle of Lake Erie was a huge victory for the Americans. They captured all the British ships. This meant the British had no way to get supplies to their troops in the West anymore. Then, Harrison pushed in from the West with his army. The British left Detroit. They went back into Canada. Things were looking good for the Americans.

Up until now, the British had also been fighting a war with Napoleon in Europe. They had not been able to give all their attention to the war in North America. However, by 1814, the British and their **allies** were close to beating Napoleon. This meant that Great Britain could send more soldiers and weapons from Europe to use in the war with the United States.

The British attacked the United States in three places. They sent troops down through Lake Champlain and along the Hudson River. They wanted to cut off New England from the rest of the United States.

The British also attacked New Orleans, in order to block the Mississippi River. The Mississippi River was very important to American trade. American **plantations** in the South shipped their goods on the river to factories in the North. The factories in the North sailed their goods back down the river to the South.

The third place the British attacked was the Chesapeake Bay. The British wanted to beat the Americans quickly. They wanted to end the war.

In July 1814, before new British soldiers arrived from Europe, American troops won a victory over the British at the Battle of Chippawa in southern Canada.

U.S. Victories at Sea

The U.S. Navy won a number of important victories over British warships during the War of 1812. Sometimes, one or two vessels from each side fought at sea. Many of these battles took place in the Atlantic Ocean, far from the United States or Great Britain.

U.S. Ship: USS *United States*

U.S. Captain: Stephen Decatur

British Ship: HMS *Macedonian*

British Captain: John Carden

Date: October 25, 1812

Location of Battle: West of the Canary Islands, near Africa

Outcome: Long-range guns on the *United States* hit the British ship more than 100 times. The *Macedonian* lost many sailors, and its masts were destroyed. The British ship surrendered.

U.S. Ship: USS *Constitution*

U.S. Captain: William Bainbridge

British Ship: HMS *Java*

British Captain: Henry Lambert

Date: December 29, 1812

Location of Battle: East coast of Brazil

Outcome: Shots from the *Constitution* knocked down the *Java*'s masts. Then, the *Java*'s own guns set the ship's sails on fire after they had fallen. After the British surrendered, American sailors destroyed the *Java* because it was so heavily damaged.

U.S. Ship: USS *Constitution*

U.S. Captain: Charles Stewart

British Ships: HMS *Cyane* and HMS *Levant*

British Captains: Gordon Thomas Falcon and George Douglas

Date: February 20, 1815

Location of Battle: Near the Cape Verde Islands, off the coast of Africa

Outcome: Before the battle, wind broke the main mast of the *Constitution*. The U.S. crew fought one British ship and then the other for two hours. The fight ended with the final U.S. victory in the War of 1812.

For a while, things looked very bad for the Americans. The British drove in through the Chesapeake Bay. Then, they marched on Washington, D.C. When they reached the city, they burned as many government buildings as they could. The Capitol Building and the president's mansion were both badly damaged.

THE WHITE HOUSE

The British entered Washington, D.C., in August 1814. Most of the 8,000 people living there had fled. First Lady Dolley Madison took a painting of George Washington off the wall of the president's mansion before fleeing to safety.

After the British burned the mansion, its walls were black from smoke. People painted it with white paint to cover the burn marks. When they had finished, the mansion was a gleaming white. That's how the building became known as the White House.

Then, the outlook changed. On September 11, 1814, the American navy destroyed the British fleet on Lake Champlain. The British pulled back. They did not want to lose more troops. Meanwhile, in Europe, in the city of Ghent, men from both sides were trying to work out an agreement. They wanted to end the war without any more fighting. They were trying to find a peaceful answer that would make everyone happy. With the British defeat on Lake Champlain, the Americans had more power to bargain for the things they wanted.

Most people had grown very tired of war. On December 24, 1814, the Americans and the British signed the **Treaty** of Ghent. The War of 1812 was over. However, the news took a long time to cross the Atlantic Ocean and reach people in America.

General Andrew Jackson was leading the American forces in the South. He had marched into Pensacola, Florida, in November. Florida was Spanish territory. British and Native American soldiers had gone there to be safe. However, Jackson went right ahead and attacked them anyway, and he won. General Jackson had then moved onward to New Orleans in December. The British soldiers there far outnumbered the Americans. Though the war was officially over, Jackson did not know this. He defeated the British at the Battle of New Orleans in January 1815.

The Battle of New Orleans was fought by about 4,500 U.S. soldiers, including a group of smugglers who hid out in the area, and 8,000 British troops.

By the terms of the Treaty of Ghent, all conquered land was to be returned to the country that controlled it before the War of 1812.

The **War of 1812** cost the United States **$105 million dollars**, an amount worth about $1.5 billion today.

The **muskets**, or guns, used in the war could fire a shot **100 yards** (91 m) at the most, so fighting took place at close range.

About **15,000** Americans and **8,600** British and Canadians **died in the War of 1812**.

Nobody really won the War of 1812. The British won some battles. The Americans won others. When it was over, things mostly went back to the way they had been before. The way Americans thought about themselves had changed, though. They had survived another war, their first as an independent country.

The Battle of New Orleans turned out to be one of the most important battles of the war. The Americans felt proud whenever they thought of the battle. American troops had fought bravely and won against bad odds.

Now, more than ever, Americans wanted to make their country bigger. They had mostly given up on spreading into Canada, but they still wanted to move west and south. To many people, taking over Florida seemed like the next step.

After his victory at New Orleans, Andrew Jackson became an American hero.

Important Places in the War of 1812

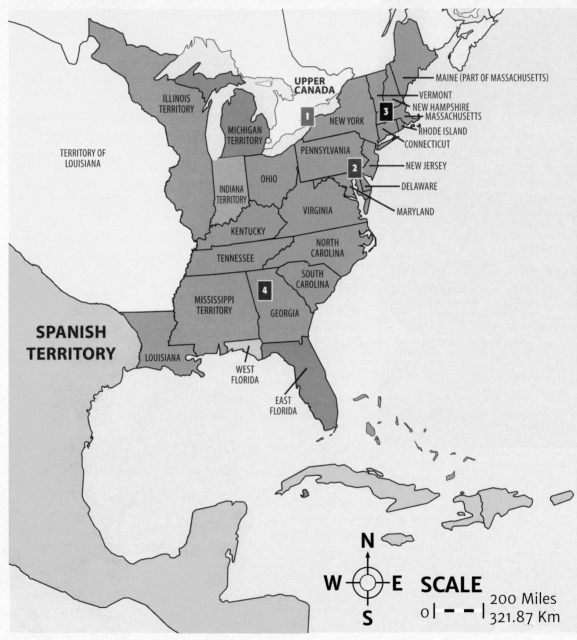

ILLINOIS TERRITORY

TERRITORY OF LOUISIANA

MICHIGAN TERRITORY

UPPER CANADA

INDIANA TERRITORY

OHIO

PENNSYLVANIA

NEW YORK

MAINE (PART OF MASSACHUSETTS)

VERMONT

NEW HAMPSHIRE
MASSACHUSETTS

RHODE ISLAND

CONNECTICUT

NEW JERSEY

DELAWARE

MARYLAND

VIRGINIA

KENTUCKY

TENNESSEE

NORTH CAROLINA

SOUTH CAROLINA

MISSISSIPPI TERRITORY

GEORGIA

SPANISH TERRITORY

LOUISIANA

WEST FLORIDA

EAST FLORIDA

N W E S

SCALE
0 — — — 200 Miles
321.87 Km

1 Fort George

Fort George was the British army's headquarters in the region called Upper Canada. In May 1813, Americans attacked the fort. They controlled it until leaving in December.

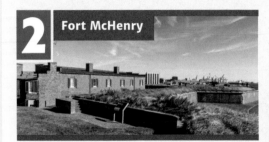

2 Fort McHenry

The Springfield Armory, in Massachusetts, was where U.S. muskets were made and repaired. The workers invented gun parts that could be changed in and out faster.

3 Springfield Armory

U.S. troops at Fort McHenry stopped an attack on Baltimore, Maryland, in September 1814. When he saw the U.S. flag still flying after the battle, Francis Scott Key wrote "The Star-Spangled Banner."

4 Horseshoe Bend National Military Park

Most Creeks, Native Americans living in what is now Georgia and Alabama, helped the British. After Andrew Jackson won a battle at Horseshoe Bend, Alabama, in 1814, the Creeks lost their land.

LEGEND

☐ Water
■ U.S. States
■ U.S. Territories
☐ Spanish Lands
☐ Other Land

Chapter Three

The Fight for Florida

In 1513, the first Europeans arrived in what is now Florida. They were Spanish. A man named Ponce de León led them. He was looking for a fountain that would make people live forever. He never found his fountain of youth. He did, however, begin the European settlement of Florida.

Before the Europeans arrived, hundreds of thousands of Native people lived in Florida. For the next 300 years, though, the French, the Spanish, and sometimes the British settled the area. As a result, Native people suffered.

As part of the 500th anniversary of Ponce de León's arrival in Florida, a copy of a 16th-century ship was displayed in several Florida cities.

Some Native Americans died in battles with the Europeans. Thousands and thousands more died from diseases that the Europeans brought with them. Some villages or Native groups were completely wiped out.

Generally, the Spanish had a friendly relationship with the Native people, though. They did not treat them as equals. However, they did not treat them as badly as many of the British settlers did.

The Spanish in Florida bought and sold both Africans and Native Americans as slaves. However, the Spanish saw slavery differently from the way the British did. Spanish slaves earned money. They were able to use their money to buy their own houses. They were also able to buy their own freedom. They did not have to remain slaves forever.

Ponce de León founded a Spanish colony in Puerto Rico before reaching Florida.

With 800 settlers, Pedro Menéndez de Avilés of Spain established the town of Saint Augustine, Florida, in 1565.

Spain created a number of settlements in Florida. They included Saint Augustine, Pensacola, and what is now called Tallahassee. The Spanish worried about the British colonies north of Florida. They were afraid the British would push them out of them. They wanted to make their colony stronger. In 1693, the Spanish offered freedom to any British slaves who went to Florida. They also welcomed Native Americans who wanted to move into Florida and settle. They hoped the African Americans and Native Americans would help them defend Florida against the British if needed.

The British were unhappy with the Spanish in Florida. They did not like that the Spanish were persuading British slaves to escape and head south. For years, the British launched attacks across the Florida border. They burned towns. They killed and captured people.

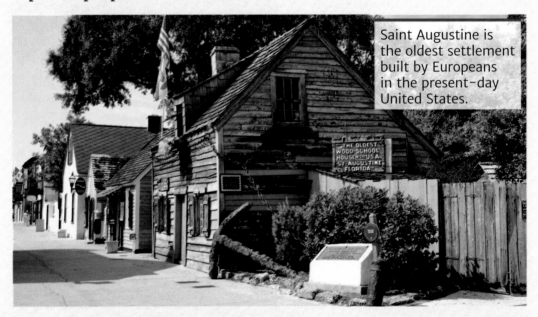

Saint Augustine is the oldest settlement built by Europeans in the present-day United States.

Then, Great Britain took control of Florida in 1763, and the tense relationship between the British and the Spanish grew worse. When the American Revolutionary War began, Spain sided with the American colonies. Spain wanted to weaken Great Britain, and Spain's efforts paid off. During the war, Spain got back part of Florida. The agreement that ended the war gave the rest back to Spain.

Though Spain had sided with the Americans, the Spanish then became nervous about their relationship with the United States. The Spanish could see that the leaders of the new country wanted more land. The Spanish did not want to lose Florida again. The people who were most nervous were the African Americans and Native Americans who lived in Florida. They knew they would lose their freedom if the Americans, who kept slaves, got control of Florida.

Completed in 1695, Castillo de San Marcos protected Saint Augustine. The fort survived attacks because the Spanish built it using a soft local stone called coquino. Cannonballs fired at the fort's walls became stuck in the soft material.

The Spanish government also worried that some of the more wealthy people in Florida might want to join the United States. So, the Spanish tried to give people reasons to stay in Florida and to like Spain. They gave businesspeople special privileges for doing business in Florida. They also offered free land to anyone who wanted to settle there. The free land attracted a lot of people.

The outcome was very different from what the Spanish had hoped. They had wanted to make Florida look like a better place, under Spanish rule, than the United States. When American settlers flooded across the border for the free land, though, Florida started to look a lot like the United States. The new settlers mainly thought of themselves as Americans. Many wanted to make Florida part of the United States. Some of them even wanted to declare independence and to rule themselves.

A fort guarded the settlement of Mobile, in present-day Alabama, when Spain controlled that area in the late 1700s and early 1800s. A copy of the fort can be seen in Mobile today.

At that time, Florida was larger than it is today. It stretched all the way to the Mississippi River. There were two parts, called East Florida and West Florida.

In 1810, the people of West Florida decided to set up their own government. They declared Baton Rouge, in what is now the state of Louisiana, as the capital. They called themselves the Republic of West Florida. They said they were now independent of Spain.

President Madison decided the United States should take advantage of the situation. He argued that West Florida was really supposed to belong to the United States. Then, the U.S. government sent troops to West Florida, and the area's leaders agreed to join the United States. The government of the Republic of West Florida was in charge of the area for just 74 days.

James Madison said that West Florida was part of the United States because it had been included in the Louisiana Purchase.

The next year, in 1811, the U.S. Congress sent American troops to fight along Florida's northern border. However, the attacks were kept a secret. If Spain got upset, Congress wanted to be able to say that it did not know about the fighting.

These attacks were mainly made against the Seminole people. The name *Seminole* came from a Spanish word meaning "runaway." White settlers had pushed many Native American groups out of Georgia and Alabama 100 years earlier. These Native Americans moved into Florida. They became known as the Seminoles or the Red Seminoles. African slaves also fled into Florida. They were known as the Black Seminoles.

In the early 1800s, many Seminole families lived in small homes called chickees. Made of logs, with a thatched roof, a chickee could be easily taken apart and carried if a family had to move quickly.

The Seminoles, especially the Black Seminoles, knew that they would lose their freedom if the United States took Florida. So, when the U.S. troops showed up, they fought as hard as they could. If they lost, they were taken to the United States. There, they were sold as slaves.

When the War of 1812 broke out, Great Britain helped the Seminoles fight the U.S. troops. Even after the war ended, though, the fighting in northern Florida continued. The Seminoles raided towns across the border in the United States. The Americans raided Seminole towns in Florida. In the decades following the War of 1812, the United States would fight a series of three wars against the Seminoles.

Osceola, a Seminole chief whose mother was Creek and whose father was British, led his people in what became known as the Seminole Wars against U.S. troops.

The conflict known as the First Seminole War was fought in 1817 and 1818. The Second Seminole War lasted from 1835 to 1842 and saw the most severe fighting. The Third Seminole War took place from 1855 to 1858.

About **2,000 U.S. soldiers** died in the **Second Seminole War**.

Spain received **$5 million** in the agreement making Florida part of the United States.

After the Seminole Wars, there were **fewer than 300 Seminoles** left in Florida.

In December 1817, General Jackson placed himself in charge of the attacks on Florida. He said that the Seminoles were dangerous. He said that Spain was too weak to control them. He used this argument as an excuse for attacking Florida.

In 1818, Jackson invaded Florida with a force of 1,800 troops. Jackson had not asked Congress for permission to attack Florida. He did not care whether Congress approved or not.

During the spring of 1818, he pushed into Florida. He and his soldiers did a lot of damage. They burned Seminole towns. Jackson arrested and killed two British men. Finally, he captured the city of Pensacola. Then, he set himself up as governor of Florida.

President James Monroe was angry at Jackson. He worried that Jackson might start another war with Great Britain and with Spain. He tried to fix the situation by giving Florida back to Spain. This shocked Jackson. The American people were not happy about this, either. Many of them thought Jackson was a hero for fighting in Florida.

Spain was getting tired of having to deal with all the trouble in Florida. The Spanish leaders saw now how easily the United States could take over. As a result, in 1819, they agreed to sell Florida to the United States.

Visitors to Florida today can watch people act out battles of the Seminole Wars.

General Jackson was still very popular with the American people. After Spain agreed to sell Florida, Jackson went on a tour around the United States to celebrate. People loved him. Finally, President Monroe gave in. He made Jackson governor of the new Florida territory.

The Seminoles were very upset. They were scared. Slavery was legal in Southern states. They knew they could lose all their freedom.

Spain had tried to protect them. The treaty that gave Florida to the United States said that everyone in Florida would have full rights and citizenship in the United States. That meant Native Americans and African Americans would have the same rights as the white people who lived there. Many Black Seminoles did not trust the treaty, though. They did not trust the United States. About 200 of them fled Florida. They moved to the Bahamas.

The Black Seminoles were right. One of the first things Jackson did was cancel the part of the treaty that gave African Americans and Native Americans citizenship. He wanted the Seminoles to leave.

Life in Florida became very hard for the Red Seminoles and Black Seminoles. People who had lived comfortable lives were now left with nothing. Anyone who was married to a black person or a Native American was also in trouble. Mixed-race people were thought of as Seminoles. Slave catchers were everywhere. Many Black Seminoles fled to Haiti or Cuba. Other Seminoles moved into wilderness areas to escape.

Jackson did not last long as governor of Florida. His wife became sick in the Florida climate. He missed his home in Tennessee. He wanted a chance to shape the United States. He was afraid he would be left out if he stayed in Florida. After less than six months as governor, Jackson quit. However, he had changed the history of Florida forever.

GET THINKING

Seeing Two Points of View

Have you ever noticed that two people can see the same person very differently? Maybe you had a teacher that you really didn't like, but your brother or sister loved him or her. Was one of you right, or were you both right? Did you just see different sides of the same person? Why do you think many Americans loved Andrew Jackson? How do you think most people described him? How do you think the Seminoles described him? Who do you think was right?

Chapter Four

American Values

The United States had been formed with a lot of good ideas. The Founding Fathers, the men who had started America, had great thoughts about what they wanted the country to be like. They wanted the country to be free. They wanted it to be able to stand on its own, without any help from other countries.

In addition, the people who gathered to write the first rules for the nation believed that people should have the right to choose their own government. This meant that people had a right to choose their leaders. They believed all white men should be equals.

Many of those Americans also believed that the United States had the right to grow larger and more powerful by taking more land. Some people worried about this kind of thinking, though. They thought that if America's borders kept getting bigger, it would not be the kind of country they wanted it to be.

By 1840, about 40 percent of Americans lived west of the Appalachians, a mountain range in the eastern United States. Each year, wagon trains carried more settlers to the West.

A country with more land would need a strong army to protect its land. It would need a strong central government. It would need more taxes to pay for the government. Many people worried that a more powerful government would be the beginning of the end

The Founding Fathers who wrote the U.S. Constitution in 1787 tried to create a strong government but also protect people's freedom.

for America. They were afraid a strong government might start to **oppress** the people. They wanted people to have an equal say, no matter whether they were poor or rich. They were afraid this might not happen if the central government made all the decisions.

Other people worried about America's growth for different reasons. They did not like when nations used force to get more land. Invading other people's land and attacking them did not seem, to them, like a good way to spread **democracy**.

When Jackson invaded Florida, Americans had different reactions. Lots of people thought he was a hero. Other people did not like what he had done. They did not like seeing the United States disrespect other people's lives. That was what Great Britain had done to them, after all.

Americans also disagreed about how the United States should treat Native Americans. Many people in the South who were not Native American supported the idea that the Native Americans should be moved out of that region. In 1829, Jackson was sworn in as president of the United States. He looked at the Native American groups, which had their own governments, as foreign nations.

Andrew Jackson used his popularity with many Americans to defeat John Quincy Adams in the presidential election of 1828.

The next year, Jackson helped pass the Indian Removal Act. This was a law that allowed the president to offer unsettled land in the West in exchange for land that Native people were living on east of the Mississippi River. Some Native Americans agreed to move to land set aside in what is now Oklahoma. Others fled into wilderness areas. About 100,000 Native Americans were forced to move. The first group removed was the Choctaw, in the winter of 1831. The Cherokee and other groups were removed later in the 1830s.

The U.S. Army marched the Native Americans more than 1,000 miles (1,600 kilometers) to their new land. Many of the marches took place in bad weather. People often did not have warm clothes. They did not have enough food to eat. Thousands of Native Americans died. They died of starvation. They died from the cold, and they died from sickness.

The journey of Cherokee and other Native people who were pushed westward under the Indian Removal Act became known as the Trail of Tears because of the people's suffering.

Some Americans were glad to see the Native Americans move west. Even before the Native Americans left, white settlers were moving in and taking over Native American property. Other Americans were horrified at the situation, though. People in the North, especially, were upset at how the Native Americans were being treated.

Many saw the Indian Removal Act as a mark of disgrace against the United States. They were upset that the U.S. government was destroying the Native Americans' way of life. Still, many Americans wanted the land on which the Native Americans were living. The marches went on, moving the Native peoples west.

American leaders started using the phrase "Manifest Destiny" to explain their actions. Something that is manifest is obvious. The term *destiny* suggests that the future is already set. So, the people using the phrase meant that they believed God wanted the United States to expand and control all the land up to the Pacific Ocean.

Graves in Brackettsville, Texas, honor Black Seminoles who escaped to Mexico but later returned to help the U.S. Army in Texas. Black Seminoles meet in the town each year to honor their history.

By spreading over the land, some people said, Americans could spread democracy. They could also spread Christianity. They could bring their way of life wherever they settled. This belief let many Americans think they had done the right thing by moving the Native peoples off their land. It took away their guilt.

Native Americans have lived in North America since **12,000 BC**.

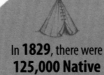

In **1829**, there were **125,000 Native Americans** living on land in the South, east of the Mississippi River.

About **15,000** Native Americans **died** during the **Trail of Tears** journey west.

The Five Civilized Tribes Museum in Oklahoma has displays about the art, history, and culture of Cherokee, Chickasaw, Choctaw, Creek, and Seminole people forced to move to the area.

The United States had started out with the idea that everyone should have freedom. By "everyone," most Americans of that time meant white men, though. Then, some people started to challenge that thinking. They started to realize that "everyone" should also mean women, African Americans, and Native people. The way people thought started to change. However, it would take a long time before new laws about equality would be passed.

From the start, many Americans had the sense that their freedoms should have no limit. They believed that America should be as big and powerful as possible. However, these ideas also led to disagreements. Americans believed in unlimited freedom, but they also believed in human rights. These same disagreements came up again and again. Americans' beliefs did not always seem to work together well. Was America's right to the land more important than the Native peoples' rights? Whose rights came first? Or did everyone have equal rights?

In 1828, Sojourner Truth became the first African-American woman to get a U.S. court to free a child slave. From then on, she preached against slavery. She also argued for giving women the same rights as men.

These were very hard questions to answer because Americans had different ways of thinking about related problems. Some people argued that Manifest Destiny meant that they were just doing what God wanted. Some white people even tried to argue that African Americans and Native Americans were not really people and did not need the same rights. Many others argued that the United States was making terrible decisions. They saw slavery and the Indian Removal Act as crimes against humanity.

These disagreements continued to shape the United States. The questions about land and human rights were argued over and over. As more settlers moved west, similar questions would come up again and again.

GET THINKING

Making Equality Work

Americans have not always lived up to the beliefs of equality and shared freedoms on which the nation was founded. Still, those beliefs have been a call to action for Americans. They have served as reminders to work hard to treat other people more fairly. They have reminded Americans to think about what is right. Sometimes, though, it has taken years for some people to change the way they live and for reality to catch up with people's beliefs. Can you think of any ways that is still true in America? Are there any groups of people today still fighting for the same rights as others?

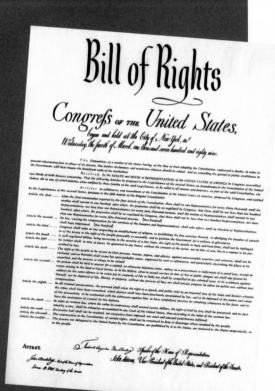

Timeline

1565—The Spanish land on the shore of the Matanzas River and found the settlement of Saint Augustine, Florida.

August 19, 1812—"Old Ironsides," the USS *Constitution*, defeats the British warship HMS *Guerriere*.

1565	1780	1790	1800

July 4, 1776—The United States declares its independence from Great Britain.

1803—Thomas Jefferson's representatives finish the Louisiana Purchase, after being sent to France to try to buy just New Orleans.

June 18, 1812—The United States declares war on Great Britain.

August 24, 1814—British troops battle with defenders outside Washington, D.C., and burn the Capitol Building, White House, Supreme Court, and Library of Congress.

1821—The treaty in which Spain gives up Florida to the United States takes effect.

1815   1825   1835   1845

1829—War hero Andrew Jackson becomes president of the United States.

1845—Florida becomes a U.S. state.

December 24, 1814—The 11 articles of the Treaty of Ghent are signed, ending the War of 1812.

Quiz

ONE
What were U.S. leaders, such as Henry Clay and Andrew Jackson, called when they pushed for the War of 1812?

TWO
What was the name of the Native American capital that Tekamthi and his brother formed in Indiana?

THREE
How many soldiers did the American army have at the start of the War of 1812?

FOUR
What did Americans call the USS *Constitution* after British cannonballs bounced off its sides?

FIVE
Which U.S. naval officer led the Battle of Lake Erie in 1813?

SIX
What river did the British hope to block by attacking New Orleans in 1814?

SEVEN
What was the name of the treaty that ended the War of 1812?

EIGHT
About how many Americans died during the War of 1812?

NINE
Which American general placed himself in charge of attacks on Florida in 1818?

TEN
What phrase did U.S. leaders use to explain their reasoning for taking land from the Native people?

Key Words

allies: groups, such as nations, that agree to fight together against enemies

democracy: a form of government in which people choose their leaders

fleet: a group of warships that travels and fights together under the command of one naval officer

hull: the main body or frame of a ship

nationalism: pride taken in belonging to a country and, sometimes, a belief that the country is better than all others

neutral: not taking sides in a war or an argument

oppress: to keep people down using force or other unfair means

plantations: large farms that grow one or a few crops intended to be sold

smuggling: moving goods secretly and often illegally into or out of an area

trade: the exchange of goods between countries

treaty: an official agreement between two or more nations

Index

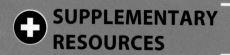

➕ SUPPLEMENTARY RESOURCES

Click on the plus icon ➕ found in the bottom left corner of each spread to open additional teacher resources.

- Download and print the book's quizzes and activities
- Access curriculum correlations
- Explore additional web applications that enhance the Lightbox experience

LIGHTBOX DIGITAL TITLES
Packed full of integrated media

VIDEOS
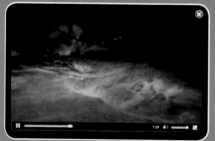

INTERACTIVE MAPS

WEBLINKS

SLIDESHOWS

QUIZZES

OPTIMIZED FOR
✔ **TABLETS**
✔ **WHITEBOARDS**
✔ **COMPUTERS**
✔ **AND MUCH MORE!**

Published by Smartbook Media Inc.
350 5th Avenue, 59th Floor
New York, NY 10118
Website: www.openlightbox.com

First published by Mason Crest in 2013

062018
121117

Library of Congress Cataloging-in-Publication Data
Names: Quinby, Michelle, author.
Title: How America became America : wars at home (1812/1820) / Michelle Quinby. Other titles: Wars at home.
Description: New York, NY : Smartbook Media Inc., [2019] | Series: How America became America | Includes index. | Audience: Grades 4-6.Identifiers: LCCN 2017054922 | ISBN 9781510535961 (hardcover : alk. paper)
Subjects: LCSH: United States--History--1809-1817--Juvenile literature. | United States--History--1817-1825--Juvenile literature. | United States--History--War of 1812--Juvenile literature. | Nationalism--United States--History--19th century--Juvenile literature. | National characteristics, American--History--19th century--Juvenile literature. | Florida--History--Cession to the United States, 1819--Juvenile literature.
Classification: LCC E341 .Q56 2018 | DDC 973.5--dc23
LC record available at https://lccn.loc.gov/2017054922

Printed in Brainerd, Minnesota, United States
1 2 3 4 5 6 7 8 9 0 22 21 20 19 18

Project Coordinator Heather Kissock
Art Director Terry Paulhus

Photo Credits
Every reasonable effort has been made to trace ownership and to obtain permission to reprint copyright material. The publisher would be pleased to have any errors or omissions brought to its attention so that they may be corrected in subsequent printings.

The publisher acknowledges Getty Images, Alamy, Newscom Shutterstock, and iStock as its primary image suppliers for this title.